WALDMAN ON DANCE

WALDMAN ON DANCE

by Max Waldman

With an Introduction by Clive Barnes

WILLIAM MORROW AND COMPANY, INC. NEW YORK/1977

ALSO BY MAX WALDMAN

Waldman on Theater

2 3 4 5 6 7 8 9 10

Library of Congress Cataloging in Publication Data

Waldman, Max.
  Waldman on dance.

  1. Dancers—Portraits.   I.   Title.
GV1785.A1W26   778.9'9'79280922   77-6627
ISBN 0-688-03227-3

Book Design by Joan Lombardi

To my brother Morris

Acknowledgments

The photographer acknowledges his debt to the gifted artists in these pages. By giving generously of their time, they gave life to a shared belief in a creative enterprise. The public little understands the enormous pressures ruling dancers' lives: there is the daily, strenuous class at the barre; studio and stage rehearsals; private coaching; and, of course, the crucial evening performance itself. In other times, a novice entering a monastic order vowed humility, poverty and chastity. Observing the disciplined existence of dancers, one might surmise that all three were still in effect to some extent—in this secular sense, that is.

Because of incessant demands on time and energy, arranging photographic sessions with dancers can become complex. Since rehearsal schedules are posted on company bulletin boards only one day in advance—and changed constantly— all plans must be made on a tentative basis. International touring commitments make many a dancer's stay in New York accountable minute by minute, precluding lengthy excursions outside the theater precincts. Then there is that ever present hazard—incapacitating injury. For this book, there were occasions when two years elapsed before our pictures were finally taken.

A dancer will arrive at the studio late in the evening, exhausted from the day's grueling work, to start once again applying full makeup and changing into costume. Not in-and-out affairs, these sittings can last as long as a full-length performance and are equally demanding. Nevertheless, the appearance of vitality becomes all the more critical here, for the photographic image remains far longer than the temporary fatigue and everything: movement and emotional intensity must be perfect. And surprisingly, all is compressed into a thimble of space—an off-square 15 by 18 feet with a ceiling ten feet high, which is low by photographic standards and for ballet, a bit ridiculous! While the dance itself is reshaped for the studio, it must be the same remembered dance. Otherwise all fails.

Such dedication to the dancing art continually evokes a sense of awe in the photographer and, in being allowed to share the mysteries of this beautiful and evanescent art, he has always felt privileged. Part of that sharing is being returned in this collection of photographs which, starting out at random, as things often do, has now become a work.

Many others have contributed: management, wardrobe, etc. Each will understand my gratitude for their concern and encouragement. Appreciation (and final curtain bouquets) to the New York State Council on the Arts' CAPS program for two grants as partial funding of this project. But first, and always first, are the dancers.

MAX WALDMAN

Sequences

**Introduction by
Clive Barnes**

Photography is the art of the instant. A moment frozen in time. A special transaction between camera and subject. A second of life selected by the photographer to represent his view of an eternity.

And dance is the art of movement through time. The most fugitive and fragile of arts, it disappears like mist on a windowpane. Who was Taglioni? Who, even, was Pavlova? Dancers tend to leave toe prints in shifting sands.

One of the difficulties inherent in capturing the live moment of dance is quite simply in the elusiveness of choreography. An actor with a written script to follow, even an opera singer with a score—all of this we can understand. But the memories of a dancer are supported with no such substructure. So we rely on film and dance notation, often in combination, to document dance. All we really get from film, though, is an indication of various aspects of a production along with some hints about the quality, if not the texture, of a performance. And dance notation, with no esthetic bias of its own, while offering a slant-free preservation of choreographic substance, merely charts the choreography. Using a scientific system of complex symbols, notation records the movement of limbs and torso. It documents the choreography so that choreographer and dancer can reconstruct the physical and spatial elements of a work. But it does not convey the phrasing, tone or texture, which is the essence of the dance.

The mystery of the performance, that chemistry between artist and audience, seems quite lost on movie film or videotape. It disintegrates. It dissipates. It fades. Dance, in a particular sense, more than any other of the theater arts is three-dimensional. Dance moves in space, and its specifically three-dimensional nature makes it almost impossible to capture either on film or television.

I have never discovered quite why this should be so. The difficulties created by the lack of a dimension are obvious. But this could surely be compensated for. After all, the art of drama is three-dimensional, too. And quite a few plays, nowadays, are taped, with little lost. But the difference is that, somehow, actors come out well on film or television. Indeed their memorial plaques are likely to be found on Sony and in color. Actors have a love affair going with a television camera that dancers do not.

Dancers are positively diminished by the moving picture. Perhaps the reason is that everything seems so naughtily easy. A film of a dancer doing spritely ballottés or thirty-two fouettés or balancing for endless moments transmits nothing of the technical difficulty of those movements. Because of the distortion of perspective imposed by the separate artistic demands of film, ethereality, sense of speed and elegance are all lost.

A student looking at Margot Fonteyn's career could, with care, reconstruct a surprising amount of documentary material. At one time or another, probably at least a third of her major roles have been committed to the movie camera. Yet, unfortunately, very little of her emerges from this film documentation. You can see something but never enough. There is, for example, a perfectly adequate film of Fonteyn in Frederick Ashton's Ondine. I would not be without it. Yet I could never recommend it as a precise evocation of an unexpectedly great performance in an unexpectedly great ballet, now both, regrettably lost.

Dance is fragile not only because it is difficult to preserve, but also because attempts to capture its magic in other media rarely succeed. There are, however, some mementos of dance that do remain pungent to memory, evocative to the senses. I never saw Isadora Duncan dance, but her way of movement has become familiar to me through the drawings of her made by José Clara. Of course these are merely individual images frozen in time, but they somehow work. In many ways they are the most eloquent record we have of the rhapsodic beauty that was Isadora's alone.

A similar wonder is performed on the Romantic ballerinas of the nineteenth century. One can read some of the most graphic descriptions of their dancing by such writers as Théophile Gautier, but it is in the lithographs of, say, Chalon, that their gifts truly come alive and their spirits are truly evoked. The important thing here is that the artist is not simply recording a fact but is able to evoke a moment. This has also been the goal of our great photographers.

Max Waldman's work in dance photography comes to us in the 1970's, although the art of dance photography extends as far back as the nineteenth century. These early pictures are absolutely fascinating. At the very least, they show what a dancer looked like and what he or she wore. But sometimes they even suggest something of the spirit of a work. The photographs of Nijinsky, for example, are extraordinarily revealing. Many people who never saw Nijinsky, and because of the brevity of his career very few people did, feel they have acquired some impression of the electrifying way he danced from pictures taken of him by photographers like de Meyer.

Originally, all dance photographs—Nijinsky's included—were studio portraits or posed stage shots. Then during the 1930's in Britain, a new trend evolved. It was called "action photography," and the purpose was to catch dancers not posing but moving in actual performance. So while the glamorous portrait photographer of dance, men such as Gordon Anthony in England and Maurice Seymour in the United States, remained, a new breed emerged, those who sat in theaters or attended rehearsals and shot dance as it happened. It is difficult to say who was the first of this new breed, but it was probably Merlyn Severn in London who, shortly before World War II, produced a book called Ballet in Action. It was a new development in ballet photography. She was followed, after the end of the war, by another two significant British photographers, Baron and Roger Wood. Also, in France, Serge Lido started to produce a series of staged action shots. Lido specialized in the kind of shot that would have a dancer disturbing the Venetian pigeons in St. Mark's Square with a temps de poisson.

With these artists a thirty-year period was launched, during which time the entire emphasis of dance photography was on performance rather than portraiture. In Europe today, most companies regularly arrange special photocalls, where the photographers can shoot away at a performance to their hearts' content. In the United States, we are poorer and less free to do the same. Union rules make it difficult to arrange special photocalls, while the European arrangement whereby a single photographer, like Anthony Crickmay, will be commissioned to cover a complete company and its repertory would here be economically unsound. Many of our companies appoint special photographers—Martha Swope, for example, for New York City Ballet, or Herbert Migdoll for the Joffrey Ballet— but these photographers are not given much latitude, because they are restricted to shooting during rehearsals and performances. All this is fine, but not always conducive to the best work.

Max Waldman, one of the most uncompromising artists I have ever encountered, found a compromise that worked in an uncompromising way. He has returned the art of dance photography from the stage to the studio, and to this controlled environment he has brought with him the tradition of the "action" photographers—the capturing of movement, not poses. The movements he captures somehow suggest both the preceding movement as well as the ones that would follow. We therefore seem to be presented with a phrase, not just a momentary image.

The incomparable Max is America's great theatrical photographer, and one of the handful of photographers who demonstrate the full range and possibility of the camera. With Max something quite fantastic happens between the subject and the camera. He developed over the years his techniques of portraiture in two major fields—the theater and the nude. His eye is as sharp as a Bill Brandt or a Brassai, and his love and knowledge of the theater enabled him to produce photographs of simply imaginative power.

A few years ago Max produced a book, Waldman on Theater, for which I also had the privilege of writing the introduction. They were really photographs that needed no introduction. Waldman's camera had penetrated to the heart of these

theatrical occasions. Interestingly he did not photograph in the theater. He broug
the theater to his studio. Here, on his own turf, he and the artists would re-create
what was, in effect, a metaphor of a performance, and this he would capture in
lens. It is a marvelous technique.

For years Max has been a devoted dance fan. He can be seen at almost every
performance of interest. So what was more likely than that he would use his own
special technique to celebrate the art of dance. The result is this fantastic and
beautiful collection of photographs.

Perhaps "celebrate" is the key word here. Max is not interested in recording
dance—or theater for that matter—but in celebrating it. He is the most astonishir
photographer. He has something of the journalistic genius of an Arnold Newman,
the special dance insight of a George Platt-Lynes, and yet also a sense of the
poetry of form that is pure Waldman. I have watched him so many times create
permanent images out of a transient reality, but I am still aghast at the knowingn
of his lens.

The pictures that follow need no words. They have their own style, their own
forcefulness. As I write, a Waldman picture of Suzanne Farrell and Peter Martins in
Jerome Robbins's Afternoon of a Faun is in my room. It is a constant evocation to
me of the harmonic elements of dance, and a constant reminder of what dance
all about— the fleeting images of remembered passion.

WALDMAN ON DANCE

Le Jeune
Homme
et la Mort

MIKHAIL BARYSHNIKOV

Other
Dances

NATALIA MAKAROVA

Studio
Improvisation

ATALIA MAKAROVA
MIKHAIL BARYSHNIKOV

Giselle

NATALIA MAKAROVA

Don Quixote

NATALIA MAKAROVA
IVAN NAGY

Chaconne

ZANNE FARRELL
TER MARTINS

Frontier
JANET EILBER

.Junk
Dances

MURRAY LOUIS

Cry

JDITH JAMISON

Grotto

GERALD OTTE
AREN SING
AMES TEETERS

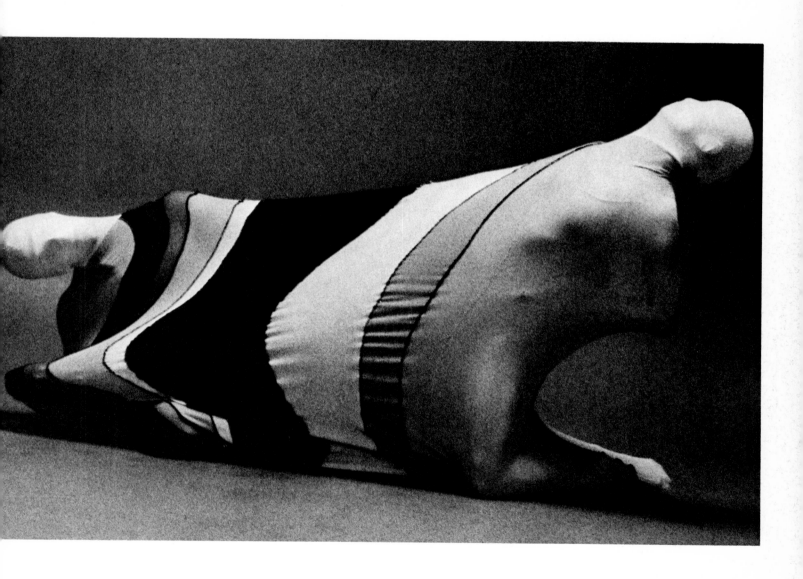

Sanctum

GERALD OTTE
KAREN SING
JAMES TEETERS

Fancy
Free
JERRY ORR

Winterbranch

CAROLYN BROWN
MERCE CUNNINGHAM

The
Cellar
MANUEL ALUM

The Moor's Pavane

CYNTHIA GREGORY
BRUCE MARKS

.Romeo
and
Juliet

GELSEY KIRKLAND
IVAN NAGY

.The
Path

PAUL SANASARDO
MICHELE REBEAUD

Jardin
Aux
Lilas

MARIANNA TCHERKASSKY
JOHN PRINZ

Les Sylphides

NATALIA MAKAROVA
VAN NAGY

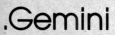

B.Lazarus

DENNIS WAYNE

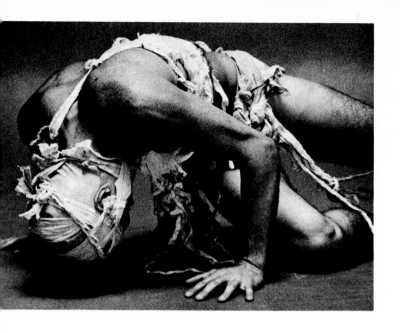

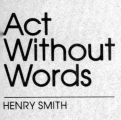

Act
Without
Words

HENRY SMITH

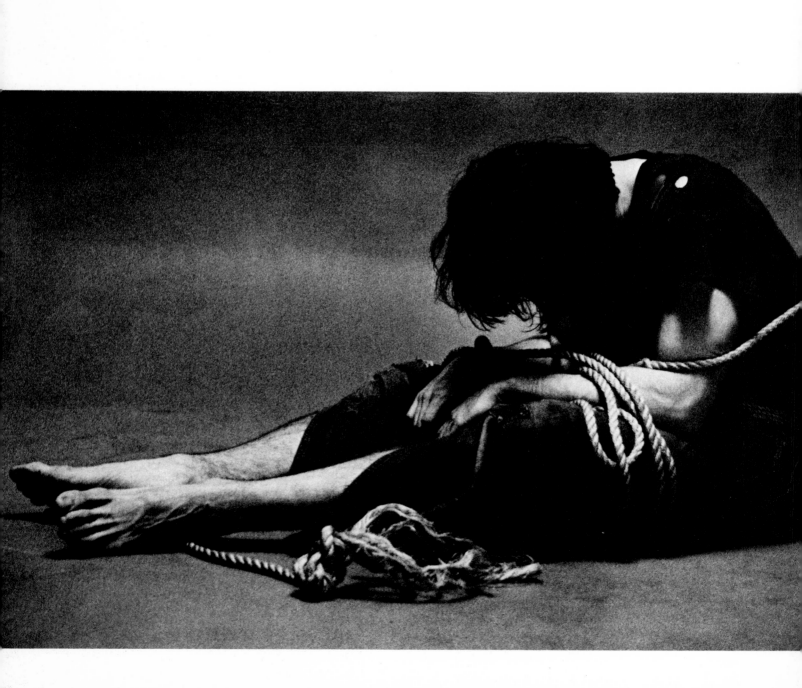

Clytemnestra

YURIKO KIMURA

Afternoon of a Faun

SUZANNE FARRELL
PETER MARTINS

Giselle

MIKHAIL BARYSHNIKOV

.The
Dying
Swan
NATALIA MAKAROVA

Title of Dance	Performed by	Choreographer	Premiere Date	Composer
1.Le Jeune Homme et la Mort (Scenario by Jean Cocteau)	Mikhail Baryshnikov	Roland Petit	1946	Johann Sebastian B
2.Other Dances	Natalia Makarova	Jerome Robbins	1976	Frederic Chopin
3.Studio Improvisation	Natalia Makarova Mikhail Baryshnikov	Studio Improvisation		
4.Giselle (Libretto: Théophile Gautier and Heinrich Heine)	Natalia Makarova	Jean Coralli Jules Perrot	1841 (Restaged: David Blair, 1968)	Adolphe Adam
5.Don Quixote (Pas de deux)	Natalia Makarova Ivan Nagy	Marius Petipa	1869	Ludwig Minkus
6.Chaconne	Suzanne Farrell Peter Martins	George Balanchine	1976	Christoph Willibald Gluck
7.Frontier	Janet Eilber	Martha Graham	1935	Louis Horst
8.Junk Dances	Murray Louis	Murray Louis	1964	Robert Wilson
9.Cry	Judith Jamison	Alvin Ailey		
10.Grotto	Gerald Otte Karen Sing James Teeters	Alwin Nikolais	1973	Alwin Nikolais
11.Sanctum	Gerald Otte Karen Sing James Teeters	Alwin Nikolais	1964	Alwin Nikolais
12.Fancy Free	Terry Orr	Jerome Robbins	1944	Leonard Bernstein
13.Winterbranch	Carolyn Brown Merce Cunningham	Merce Cunningham	1964	La Monte Young
14.The Cellar	Manuel Alum	Manuel Alum	1967	W. Kilar
15.After Eden	Alba Calzada Lawrence Rhodes	John Butler	1967	Lee Hoiby

Selection	Costumes	Production by	Photographed	Date
Passacaglia	Christian Bèrard	American Ballet Theatre	New York	1975
1 Waltz; 4 Mazurkas	Santo Loquasto	American Ballet Theatre	New York	1976
			New York	1974
Original Score	Paul Lormier (Peter Hall, 1968)	American Ballet Theatre	New York	1970
Don Quixote Pas de deux		American Ballet Theatre	New York	1972
Orpheus and Eurydice	Karinska	New York City Ballet	New York	1976
Original Score	Martha Graham	Martha Graham Dance Company	New York	1976
Original Score	Frank Garcia	Murray Louis Dance Company	New York	1976
		Alvin Ailey City Center Dance Theatre	New York	1976
Original Score	Alwin Nikolais	Nikolais Dance Theatre	New York	1976
Original Score	Alwin Nikolais	Nikolais Dance Theatre	New York	1976
Original Score	Kermit Love	American Ballet Theatre	New York	1976
Two Sounds (1960)	Robert Rauschenberg	Merce Cunningham and Dance Company	New York	1970
Dipthongos	Manuel Alum	Manuel Alum Dance Company	New York	1969
Original Score	David Murin	Pennsylvania Ballet	New York	1976

Title of Dance	Performed by	Choreographer	Premiere Date	Composer
16.The Moor's Pavanne (Variations on a Theme of Othello)	Cynthia Gregory Bruce Marks	José Limon	1949	Henry Purcell
17.Giselle (Libretto: Théophile Gautier and Heinrich Heine)	Carla Fracci Paolo Bortoluzzi	Jean Coralli Jules Perrot	1841 (Restaged: David Blair, 1968)	Adolphe Adam
18.Romeo and Juliet	Gelsey Kirkland Ivan Nagy	Kenneth MacMillan	1943	Serge Prokofiev
19.The Path (Section: Ice)	Paul Sanasardo Michèle Rebeaud	Paul Sanasardo	1972	Steve Drews
20.Jardin Aux Lilas	Marianna Tcherkassky John Prinz	Antony Tudor	1938	Ernest Chaussc
21.Les Sylphides	Natalia Makarova Ivan Nagy	Michel Fokine	1907	Frederic Chopi.
22.Gemini	Martine Van Hamel Jolinda Menendez Clark Tippet Charles Ward	Glen Tetley	1973	Hans Werner Henze
23.Lazarus	Dennis Wayne	Norman Walker	1973	Lubos Fiser
24.Act Without Words	Henry Smith	Anna Sokolow	1971	Joel Thome
25.Clytemnestra	Yuriko Kimura	Martha Graham	1958	Halin El-Dabh
26.Afternoon of a Faun	Suzanne Farrell Peter Martins	Jerome Robbins	1953	Claude Debussy
27.Giselle (Libretto: Théophile Gautier and Heinrich Heine)	Mikhail Baryshnikov	Jean Coralli Jules Perrot	1841 (Restaged: David Blair, 1968)	Adolphe Adam
28.The Dying Swan	Natalia Makarova	Michel Fokine	1907	Saint-Saëns

Selection	Costumes	Production by	Photographed	Date
Derived from various selections	Pauline Lawrence	American Ballet Theatre	New York	1972
Original Score	Paul Lormier (Peter Hall, 1968)	American Ballet Theatre	New York	1976
Original Score	Eugene Berman	American Ballet Theatre	New York	1976
Original Score "Ice"	Paul Sanasardo	Sanasardo Dance Company	New York	1976
Poème	Raymond Sovey (After sketches by Hugh Stevenson)	American Ballet Theatre	New York	1976
Based on piano pieces		American Ballet Theatre	New York	1970
Third Symphony	Nadine Baylis	American Ballet Theatre	New York	1976
Original Score	David James	DANCERS	New York	1976
Original Score	Anna Sokolow	Anna Sokolow's Players Project	New York	1972
Original Score	Martha Graham	Martha Graham Dance Company	New York	1974
Original Score	Irene Sharaff	New York City Ballet	New York	1976
Original Score	Paul Lormier (Peter Hall, 1968)	American Ballet Theatre	New York	1975
"Swan" from the Carnival of Animals		American Ballet Theatre	New York	1970